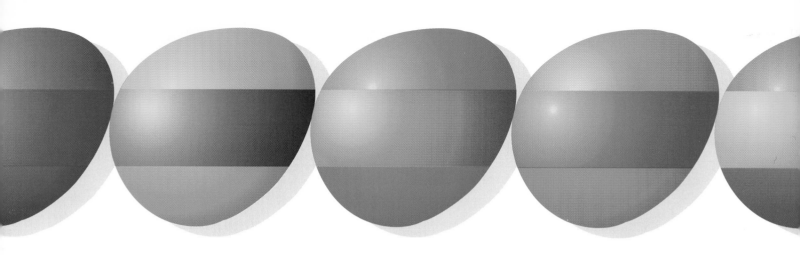

THE CHILD'S WORLD

EASTER
CRAFTS

by Jean Eick

Library of Congress Cataloging-in-Publication Data
Eick, Jean. 1947-
Easter Crafts / by Jean Eick.
p. cm.
Includes index.
Summary: Includes lists of things needed and specific directions
for making a variety of crafts related to Easter.
ISBN 1-56766-536-5 (library bound : alk. Paper)

1. Easter decorations — Juvenile literature.
2. Handicraft — Juvenile literature.
[1. Easter decorations. 2. Handicraft.]
I. Title.

TT900.E2E35 1998   98-13108
745.594'1 — dc21   CIP
                                                          AC

GRAPHIC DESIGN & ILLUSTRATION
Robert A. Honey, Seattle

PRODUCTION COORDINATION
James R. Rothaus / James R. Rothaus & Associates

ELECTRONIC PRE-PRESS PRODUCTION
Robert E. Bonaker / Graphic Design & Consulting Company

CONTENTS

1 For many people, Easter is a very special holiday. It's a day full of happiness and laughter. It's also a day to celebrate life. This book is full of fun Easter ideas for you to make and do. By carefully reading and following the directions, you'll soon have lots of Easter crafts around your house.

2 Before you start making any craft, be sure to read the directions. Make sure you look at the pictures too, they'll help you understand what to do. Go through the list of things you'll need and get everything together. When you're ready, find a good place to work. Now you can begin making your crafts.

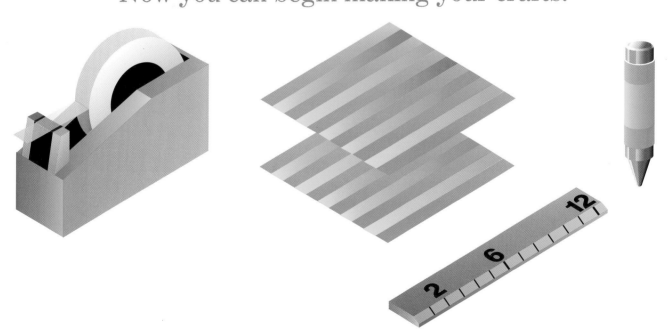

You can make lots of pretty eggs to put up almost anywhere.

PAPER EGGS

Things You'll Need

Scissors.

Construction Paper in Light Colors.

Glue. *Pencil.*

1 Draw an egg on a piece of construction paper.

Trace me.

2 Carefully cut it out with scissors.

Things for Decorating

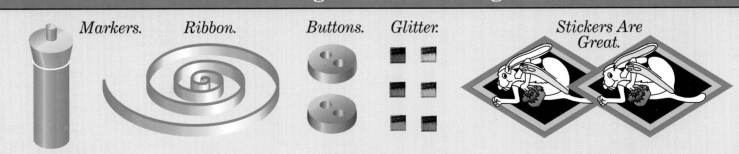

Markers. *Ribbon.* *Buttons.* *Glitter.* *Stickers Are Great.*

3 Decorate the egg anyway you like. Apply stickers.

4 Or put glue on the egg and sprinkle glitter on it.

5 Or do some wild art with colored markers.

6 Or glue wrapping paper to the paper egg and edge it with white tape.

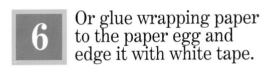

You can make lots of pretty eggs to put up almost anywhere.

EGG STRINGS

Things You'll Need

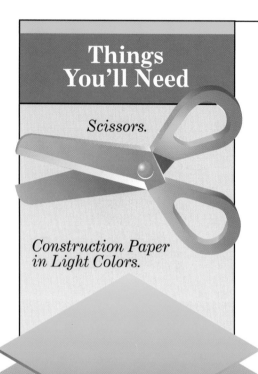

Scissors.

Construction Paper in Light Colors.

A Cookie Cutter Shaped Like An Egg.

Pencil.

1 Use the cookie cutter, or trace the pattern on page 8, to draw an egg shape on one end of a piece of paper. Make sure the paper is long enough for 3 more egg shapes.

The edge of the egg shape should slightly hang over the end of the paper.

Things for Decorating

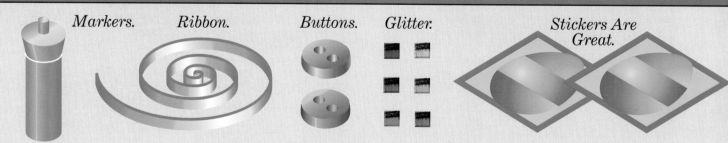

Markers.   *Ribbon.*   *Buttons.*   *Glitter.*   *Stickers Are Great.*

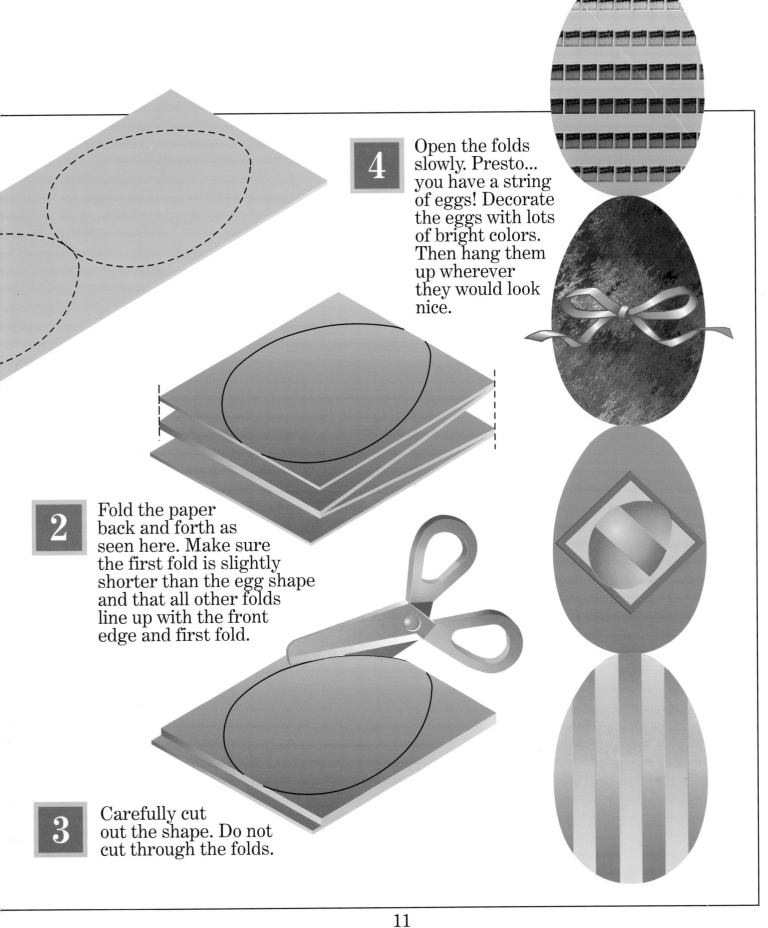

4 Open the folds slowly. Presto... you have a string of eggs! Decorate the eggs with lots of bright colors. Then hang them up wherever they would look nice.

2 Fold the paper back and forth as seen here. Make sure the first fold is slightly shorter than the egg shape and that all other folds line up with the front edge and first fold.

3 Carefully cut out the shape. Do not cut through the folds.

Everyone can make one of these bunnies to decorate.

BUNNY

Things You'll Need

Scissors.

White Paper Plate.

Pink Construction Paper.

Black Marker.

Glue.

Yarn, String, or Narrow Ribbon.

3 Cotton Balls.

Pink Pom Pom.

1

Use the marker to draw a face on the plate.

2

Glue the cotton balls and pom pom to the plate.

3 Cut the ears from the construction paper.

4 Glue the ears to the back. Add yarn to hang.

These gifts make nice Easter surprises for your friends or teachers.

BUNNY BASKET

Things You'll Need

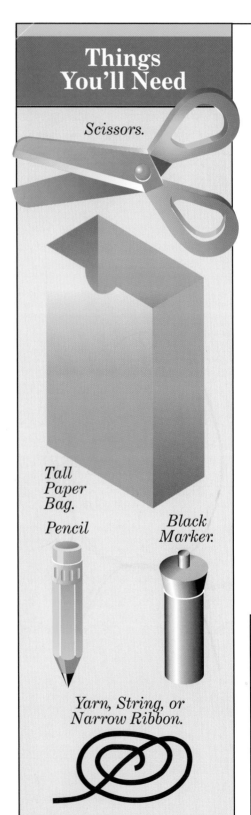

Scissors.

Tall Paper Bag.

Pencil

Black Marker.

Yarn, String, or Narrow Ribbon.

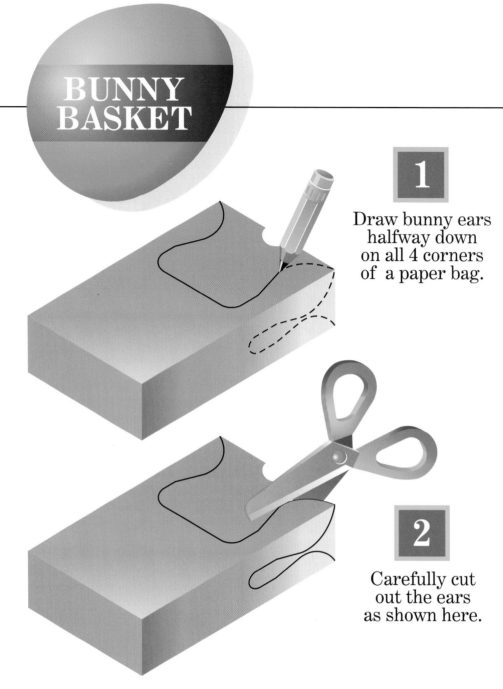

1

Draw bunny ears halfway down on all 4 corners of a paper bag.

2

Carefully cut out the ears as shown here.

Things for Decorating

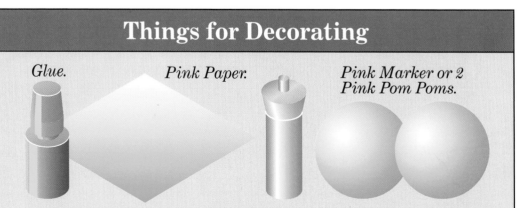

Glue.

Pink Paper.

Pink Marker or 2 Pink Pom Poms.

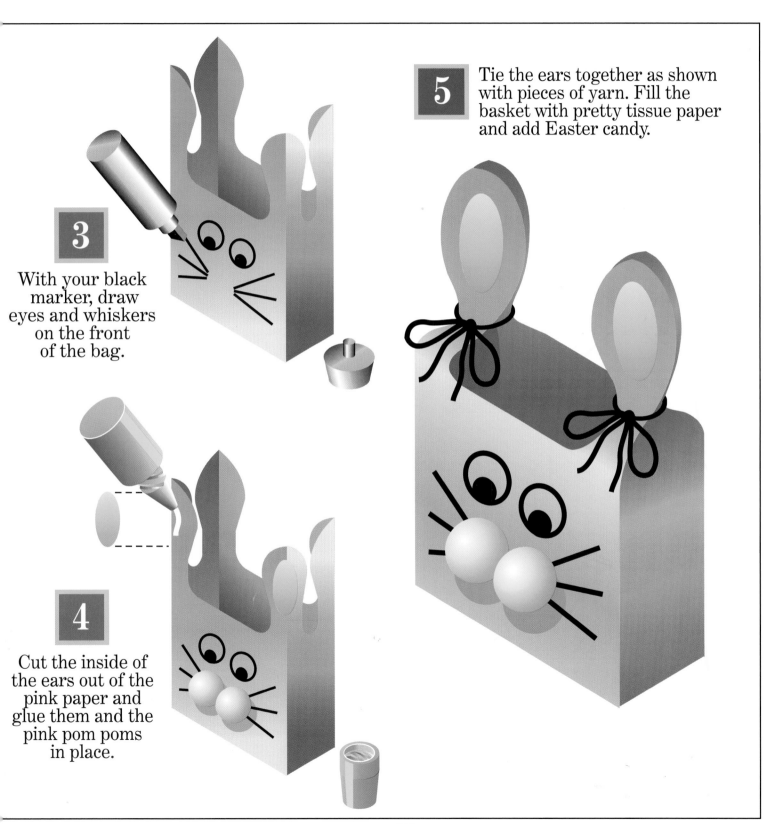

3

With your black marker, draw eyes and whiskers on the front of the bag.

4

Cut the inside of the ears out of the pink paper and glue them and the pink pom poms in place.

5

Tie the ears together as shown with pieces of yarn. Fill the basket with pretty tissue paper and add Easter candy.

These holders are a great way to show off your Easter eggs.

EGG HOLDERS

Things You'll Need

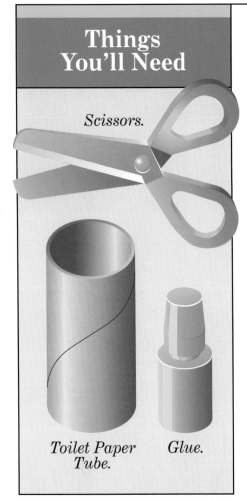

Scissors.

Toilet Paper Tube.

Glue.

1 Lay the tube flat. Use the scissors to cut the tube in half.

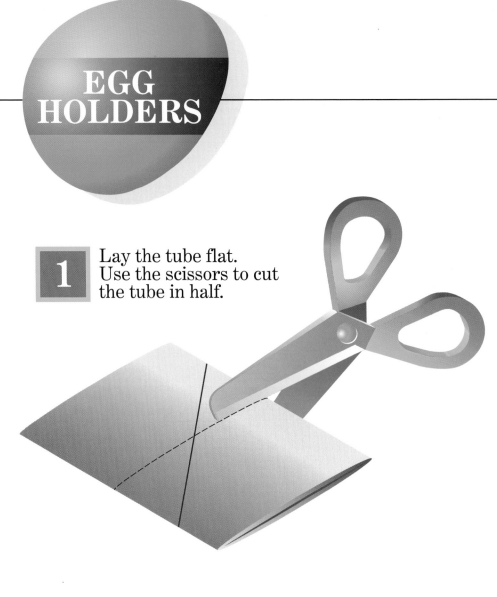

Things for Decorating

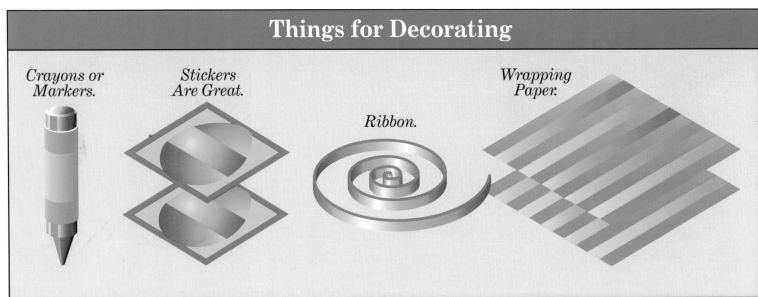

Crayons or Markers.

Stickers Are Great.

Ribbon.

Wrapping Paper.

2 Cut a piece of paper as wide as the tube. Make sure the paper is three times longer than the tube is wide.

3 Glue the paper to the tube. Trim off any extra paper with your scissors.

4 Create your own designs or paste objects on the tube.

5 Place an Easter egg on top of the holder.

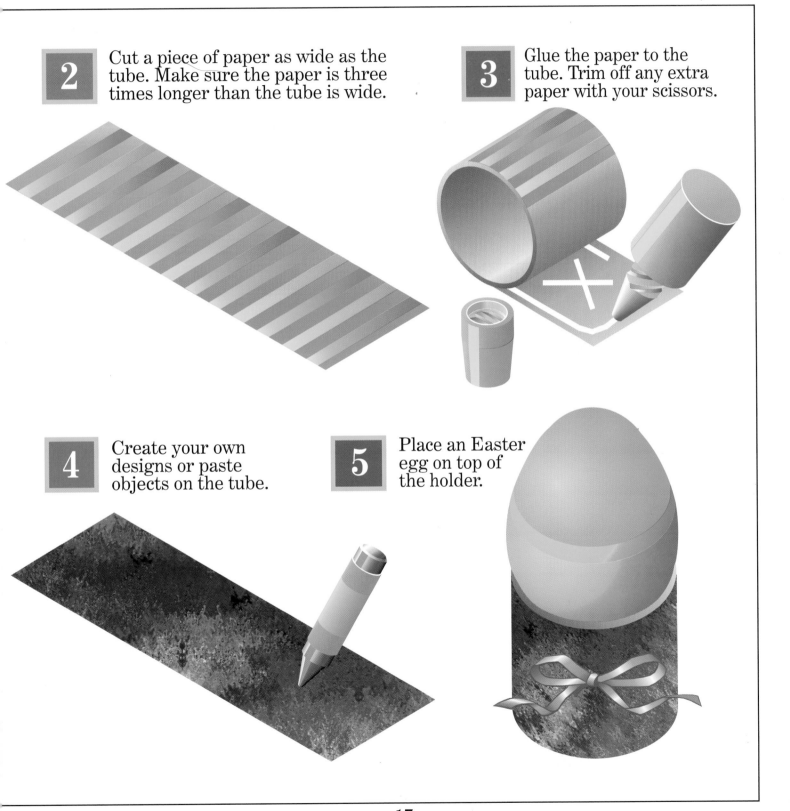

Many people like to send Easter cards to their friends and family. Now you can make your own cards.

CARDS

Things You'll Need

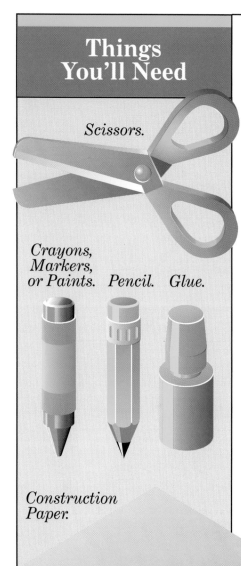

Scissors.

Crayons, Markers, or Paints. *Pencil.* *Glue.*

Construction Paper.

1 Fold the paper to the size you want your card to be. Folding it once will make a large card.

2 Folding it twice will make a small card.

3 Decorate the front of the card.

4 Write a message on the inside of the card. You can decorate the inside, too. Don't forget to sign your name.

Things for Decorating

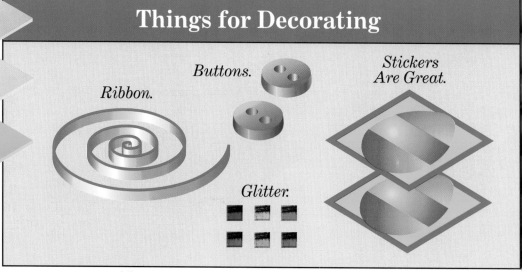

Ribbon. *Buttons.* *Stickers Are Great.*

Glitter.

Instead of making a square card, make one shaped like a Easter egg!

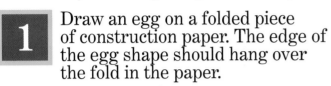

1 Draw an egg on a folded piece of construction paper. The edge of the egg shape should hang over the fold in the paper.

2 Carefully cut out the shape. Do not cut through the fold.

3 Now open the card. You should see two Easter egg shapes.

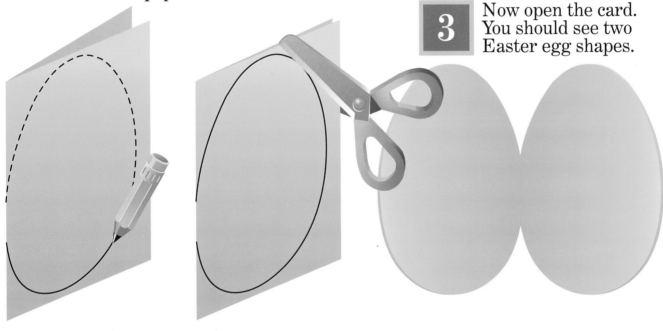

? Cut out magazine pictures that remind you of Easter and glue them to your cards. Things such as flowers, baby animals, and clouds make nice decorations.

19

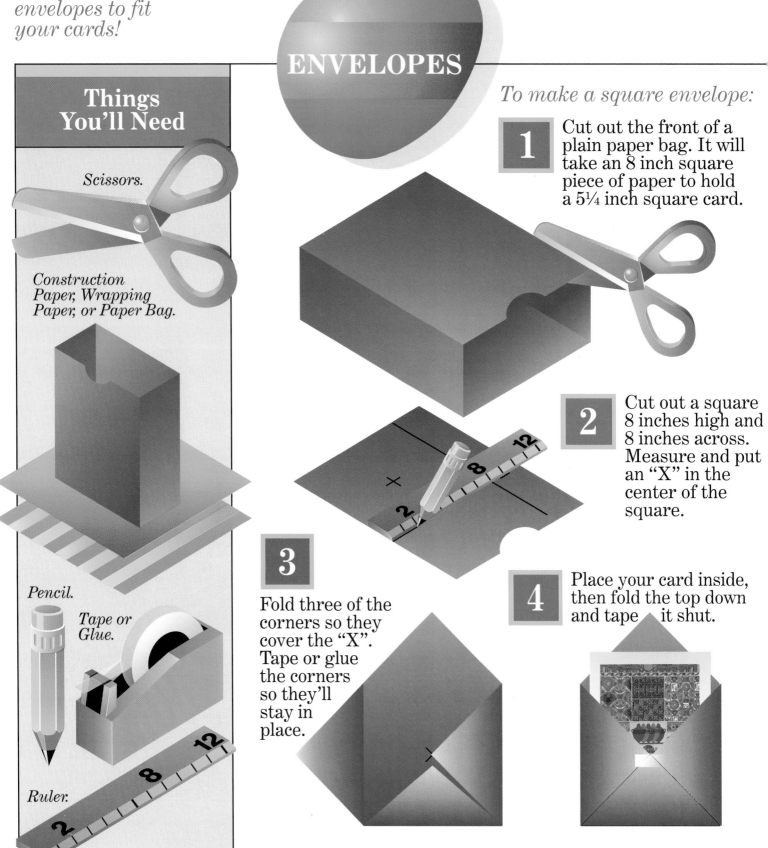

You can even make your own envelopes to fit your cards!

ENVELOPES

Things You'll Need

Scissors.

Construction Paper, Wrapping Paper, or Paper Bag.

Pencil.

Tape or Glue.

Ruler.

To make a square envelope:

1 Cut out the front of a plain paper bag. It will take an 8 inch square piece of paper to hold a 5¼ inch square card.

2 Cut out a square 8 inches high and 8 inches across. Measure and put an "X" in the center of the square.

3 Fold three of the corners so they cover the "X". Tape or glue the corners so they'll stay in place.

4 Place your card inside, then fold the top down and tape it shut.

To make an envelope that isn't square:

1 If your card is 4 inches wide, you will need paper that is: 4+4+1, or 9 inches wide. The height of the paper should be 4 inches taller than your card. Draw a line 2 inches down from the top.

2 Fold the top down along the line.

3 Place your card under the flap with the top against the fold line.

4 Fold in each side over the card.

5 Fold up the bottom of the card.

6 Before you glue the envelope together, Take out the card.

7 Glue the sides of the envelope together, stopping at the top fold.

8 Fold up and glue the bottom of the envelope.

9 Put your card back inside. Fold down the top and glue or tape the envelope shut.

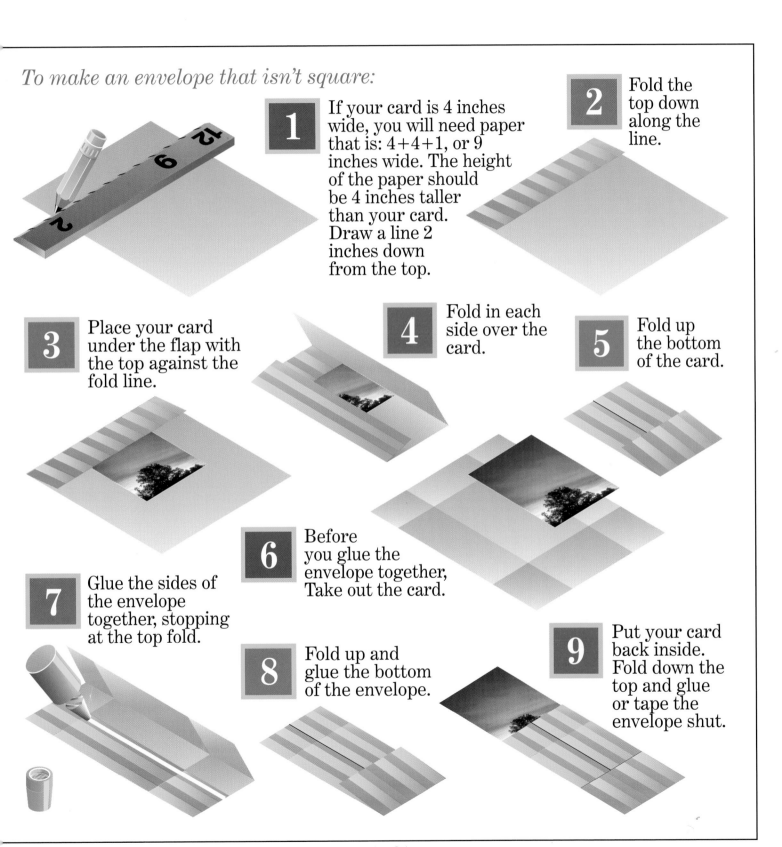

ACTIVITIES

1 Hold an egg decorating party. Invite your friends over to decorate some hard-boiled eggs an adult has cooked for you. Have each person bring something to decorate the eggs, such as crayons or cloth.

2 Start an outdoor garden. Plant some seeds inside a pot or a small container. Water the seeds and give them plenty of sunlight every day. When the seeds are ready, take the pot outside. Then plant the seeds in a garden or flowerbed.

3 Hold an Easter parade. Wear fancy hats and dress up with your friends. Then show your parents how nice you look.

4 Have an egg-and-spoon race in your yard. Give everyone a spoon and a hard-boiled egg that is still in its shell. Have everyone hold their spoons in their hands. Then tell everyone to put the eggs on the spoons. Then have everyone line up for a race. The winner is the first person to get to the finish line without dropping the egg off the spoon!